The Art of
HENRY O. TANNER
(1859-1937)

81. *Portrait of Henry O. Tanner*, 1900, by Thomas Eakins   Hyde Collection, Glens Falls, N

The Art of
HENRY O. TANNER
(1859-1937)

Organized by the Frederick Douglass Institute

in collaboration with the

National Collection of Fine Arts

Smithsonian Institution

8th and G Streets, NW

City of Washington

Exhibition Schedule

Contents

Foreword

With this exhibition of the art of Henry O. Tanner, the
Frederick Douglass Institute, in collaboration with the
National Collection of Fine Arts, provides the first real
opportunity for the American public to become acquainted
with the work of an important American expatriate artist
of the late 19th and early 20th centuries.

This introduction to Tanner, probably the most
important Afro-American artist in the nation's history,
comes at a time when there is vital new interest in the
contribution of Afro-Americans to the life and culture of
the United States.

It is the purpose of the Frederick Douglass Institute,
together with its companion Museum of African Art, to
portray the rich creative heritage of the Afro-American and
African peoples. But the young institute could not have
undertaken the task of organizing a national exhibition at
this time without the generous assistance of the National·
Collection of Fine Arts and of the Smithsonian Institution
whose policy it is to lend facilitative support to small
museums. Many hands, representing both the public and
private sectors, have in fact joined to make this exhibition
possible.

The project has been carried out by a joint museum committee composed of Mrs. Adelyn Breeskin, Harry Lowe, David Scott, and Robert Tyler Davis of the National Collection of Fine Arts and by Carroll Greene, Jr., and the undersigned representing the Frederick Douglass Institute.

The Smithsonian Institution Traveling Exhibition Service under Mrs. Dorothy Van Arsdale is arranging for a national tour of the exhibition following its opening in Washington.

Anders Richter, director of the Smithsonian Press, has rendered invaluable assistance in the preparation and publication of the catalogue.

The exhibition originated at the initiative of Mr. Greene, a trustee of the Frederick Douglass Institute and curator of its Afro-American Collection, who currently serves as a Research Associate at the Smithsonian Institution. Learning that some 200 of Tanner's paintings and studies were being made available in America by the artist's son, Jesse Tanner, he urged that a group of these be kept intact and accessible to scholars and to the public.

Accordingly, fifty oils, watercolors, drawings, and etchings—the largest single collection in existence—were acquired on behalf of the Frederick Douglass Institute by Mr. and Mrs. Norman B. Robbins of Worcester, Massachusetts. Thirty-five of these works from the artist's personal collection comprise the nucleus of the present show, to which some twenty-five museums and individuals from throughout the United States have lent other major works.

The sale of Tanner's studio collection was handled by Grand Central Art Galleries in New York whose director, Erwin S. Barrie, was Tanner's friend and patron for many years, as well as his dealer. To Mr. Barrie and to Jesse Tanner, a French citizen, we extend our thanks for their advice and for the donation of important photos, documents, awards, and medals which provide historical background for the collection and exhibit.

We wish to express gratitude to Mr. and Mrs. Robbins for the public service they have rendered in acquiring the special Tanner collection and to all of the institutions and individuals who have lent works to the show, especially to Mrs. Sadie T. M. Alexander, the artist's niece.

For financial support we are particularly indebted to the National Endowment for the Humanities, the Samuel H. Kress Foundation, and the Smithsonian Institution, as well as to the museums participating in the national tour.

Finally we wish to acknowledge the many contributions made to the actual organization of the exhibition. Robert Hilton Simmons served, together with Mr. Greene, as co-organizer, researching and gathering many of the art works, arranging for the restoration and reframing of those paintings and drawings which were in disrepair and preparing much of the catalogue. Particular thanks must go to those members of the staffs of the NCFA and the Smithsonian who have generously given of their time and specialized skills in the preparation of the exhibition and catalogue, especially to Oliver Anderson, Miss Stephanie Belt, Miss Katherine Kirk, Mrs. Valma Foster, Chris Karras, Miss Georgia Rhoades, and John Walker.

Warren M. Robbins
Founder and Director
Frederick Douglass Institute—Museum of African Art

Lenders to the Exhibition

Mrs. Sadie T. M. Alexander, Philadelphia, Pennsylvania

American National Red Cross, Washington, D. C.

Art Institute of Chicago, Illinois

Mr. and Mrs. Erwin S. Barrie, Greenwich, Connecticut

Isaac Delgado Museum of Art, New Orleans, Louisiana

Frederick Douglass Institute, Washington, D. C.

Collection of Mr. and Mrs. Norman B. Robbins

Fisk University Department of Art, Nashville, Tennessee

Grand Central Art Galleries, New York, New York

Mr. Carroll Greene, Jr., Washington, D. C.

Hampton Institute, Hampton, Virginia

High Museum of Art, Atlanta, Georgia

Howard University Gallery of Art, Washington, D. C.

Hyde Collection, Glens Falls, New York

Mrs. Salim Lewis, New York, New York

Los Angeles County Museum of Art, Los Angeles, California

Mr. Thomas Loguidice, New York, New York

Mrs. Marcia M. Mathews, Atlanta, Georgia

Milwaukee Art Center, Milwaukee, Wisconsin

Museum of Art, Carnegie Institute, Pittsburgh, Pennsylvania

Museum of Fine Arts, Houston, Texas

Pennsylvania Academy of the Fine Arts, Philadelphia, Pennsylvania

Philadelphia Museum of Art, Philadelphia, Pennsylvania

Mr. Warren M. Robbins, Washington, D. C.

Mr. and Mrs. Henry W. Sawyer III, Philadelphia, Pennsylvania

Mr. Merton D. Simpson, New York, New York

Spelman College, Atlanta, Georgia

Mr. Jesse O. Tanner, Paris, France

Mr. Haig Tashjian, New York, New York

Introduction

The continually changing vogues in art during the last quarter century are reminiscent of the rapid succession of the art movements in Paris in the early 1900s. But while new experiments in art increase today, important artists of the past are also being brought again to the forefront, allowing them to be re-assessed in a freer atmosphere by a broader and more sophisticated public. In this fertile period of rediscovery, the exemplary life and work of Henry Ossawa Tanner merit renewed recognition.

Tanner spent most of his life as an artist in Paris. But even before he left America, his immense talent was recognized by his revered teacher Thomas Eakins with whom he studied at the Pennsylvania Academy of the Fine Arts. Later, Eakins paid him the considerable tribute of painting his portrait (frontispiece).

Henry O. Tanner was a man of independent mind and vision. He remained aloof from the post-impressionists and from the abstract movement of his time, as did many of his contemporaries. And yet, he was enthusiastically acclaimed by the French art critics and was elected by the French government as a Chevalier of the Legion of Honor.

In the United States his name has been nearly forgotten by all except a few collectors, museum specialists, and a cadre of his fellow Afro-Americans who have always taken a very understandable pride in his achievement.

Although the largest number of Tanner's works are Biblical, one would be misled to think of him merely as a religious painter. Undoubtedly, his religious upbringing (his father was a prominent bishop) gave him an unusual familiarity with Biblical events and characters. But we feel even in his genre paintings and landscapes his passion for that elusive mystical element in life. Perhaps even his Biblical works are more mystical than conventionally religious in feeling. The mature Tanner arrived at his own personal religion while retaining a profound respect for the mysteries of man's existence.

In a recent letter to the Frederick Douglass Institute, Jesse O. Tanner writes: "The public . . . wanted to see every button on the coat. My father wanted the public to commune with the picture and the subject, and everybody was expected to bring something out of themselves."

In order for the viewer to do this, he must stand off from most of Tanner's works, especially his paintings, which are not intended for close viewing. A close viewing does, however, reveal his skillfully subtle blending of diverse colors and an economy of brushstrokes to achieve a harmonious result. Persons are often represented as mere brushstrokes on his canvasses, but they emerge as humans as we stand off from them. We recall that the artist frequently posed his models in an adjoining room at some distance from himself while he painted them from his studio. The contrasting of light and dark, the transforming effects of light on color were special challenges to him as he developed his personal style and technique.

Tanner's colors, it has been observed, are usually those of the late afternoon, dusk, and evening. His use of blues is striking whether in his earlier works or the later paintings of blue/green tones which predominate after about 1905.

Tanner's subjects are usually active people. They must be doing something, going to or coming from some place. When not painting friends or members of his family, he invariably depicts the simple folk; the blacks of the American South, the faces of Jerusalem and North Africa, or the fishermen at Etaples—the gentle, unaffected people. His study of Jesus becomes Our Savior, not Our Lord, and in this remarkable painting (cat. 37) he avoids both pietism and sentimentalism. One feels that this man would indeed "lay down his life for his friend." In Tanner's people there is no hubris, but a beauty in simplicity and the intuitive knowledge that human life can never be lived or explained in scientific drama alone. There must be the indefinable mystical element.

Tanner was a very painstaking artist. He worked slowly and methodically in the development of his unusual glazing technique. The glazed works have a strikingly Romantic quality not unlike that of Ryder. Almost vehement in his rejection of Post-Impressionism, he allowed his palette to be considerably lightened by the impact of Impressionism.

Tanner's attempt over the years to perfect a personal style and technique is startlingly revealed in his drawings, watercolors, prints, and paintings done between 1881 and 1936. More than an artist's work is shown here for the life of Tanner is inextricable from his work.

This exhibition coming some three decades after the artist's death is an affirmation that Henry O. Tanner belongs to the Nation. Hopefully, it will serve as a long overdue "welcome home" to a remarkable native son.

Carroll Greene, Jr.

I wish to express my personal appreciation to Charles Blitzer, Assistant Secretary for History and Art, and to Frank A. Taylor, Director-General of Museums, Smithsonian Institution, who, during my period of research under their auspices, have generously encouraged and supported the efforts to bring this exhibition to fruition.

C.G.

HENRY OSSAWA TANNER:
Selections from his Writings

The World's Work,
volume 18 (June 1909)

My recollections of Pittsburgh, Pa., where I was born, and
which I left at about five years of age, are confined
singularly enough to the memory of a great Dutch oven.
That all the other things, or nearly all, have vanished from
my memory makes one inquire, why? What was it that so
indelibly impressed this cumbersome structure upon a
childish mind? Was it the flames licking the interior with
their serpent-like shapes—caged lurid serpents—seeking,
as it were, a means of escape, but whose brilliancy faded
into wreathing smoke when their over-leaping desire
carried them too far from their source of life? Or was it
the great brown savory loaves, the crumpled edges of
which always fell to our lot. Was it the artistic sense of the
weird, or was it more probably the mere prospect of
"loaves and fishes"?

Aside from any personal memories, Pittsburgh has
always been dear to me because of hearing my father say
so many times, "A Pittsburgher of three generations." We
children came to know that this expression was the one
often used after his "fur had been rubbed the wrong way."

There was always a touch of pride in it, and I soon got to feel that "a Pittsburgher of three generations" was a thing that did not fall to the lot of every man. "Like father, like son." Once in my life (once only, I believe) I was heard to say "A Pittsburgher of four generations."

My early years, as I recollect, ran the usual course of childish vicissitudes; but, when I had become a lad of twelve or thirteen, there occurred a trivial event which was to me of the utmost importance. I was walking out with my father one fine afternoon in Fairmount Park, Philadelphia, where we then resided, when I saw for the first time a real, live artist—and at work.

The subject the artist had chosen was a middle distance hillside with a magnificent elm in bold relief. Showing my lack of comprehension of what the artist was trying to do, I asked my father: "Why does he not have a spy-glass so that he can see that big tree more distinctly? Why does he get so far away?" It was this simple event that, as it were, set me on fire. Like many children, I had drawn upon my slate to the loss of my lessons, or all over the fences to the detriment of the landscape, but never had it crossed my mind that I should be an artist, nor had I ever wished to be. But, after seeing this artist at work for an hour, it was decided on the spot, by me at least, that I would be one, and I assure you it was no ordinary one I had in mind.

The securing of colors and brushes was not so simple a matter—they had to be bought. I was one of a large family, and my father, a minister in the African Methodist Episcopal Church, was in the throes of buying a home. However, a long conversation with my mother that night produced fifteen cents, and this, early the next morning, secured from a common paint shop some dry colors and a couple of scraggy brushes. Then I was out immediately for a sketch. I went straight to the spot where I had seen the artist of the day before. Don't you suppose a boy, trying to hold a canvas between his knees and mix dry colors upon a pasteboard palette, might be liable to get things mixed? Well, I did. Whether I got the most of the paint upon the

15

canvas, upon myself, or upon the ground, it would be hard to tell. But that I was happy, supremely so, there was no doubt. Coming home that night, I examined that sketch from all points of view, upside down, and down side up, decidedly admiring and well content with my first effort. There was one little disconcerting fact, however—it seemed best upside down!

From this time forward, I was all aglow with enthusiasm, working spare times between school hours, and it soon became the talk of the school—naturally helped on by my boasting—that I was going to be an artist. The taunt of some—"An artist! he is always poor and dies in a garret!" —had no depressing effect upon me. I was not going to be that kind of an artist—not one of your "every day kind"; and off I was to my kingdom in the clouds.

During one of my school vacations, I had worked and saved fifty dollars. This was to be devoted to study. But with whom should I study? No man or boy to whom this country is a land of "equal chances" can realize what heartaches this question caused me, and with what trepidation and nervousness I made the round of the studios. The question was not, would the desired teacher have a boy who knew nothing and had little money, but would he have *me,* or would he keep me after he found out who I was? I went to Mr. M———. He "had other pupils!" Finally, Mr. I. L. Williams agreed to take me for two dollars a lesson. I was so excited that I could hardly wait for the appointed day to arrive. What a wonderland his studio was to me! I was dazzled; dazed by the thought that I was at last to be the pupil of an artist; what astonishing progress I should make! How I should strive, in a few lessons, to overtake his one other pupil! I dreamed of it by night, and my day-dreams were not less vivid.

The day or two of waiting did pass, and I was on hand long before the appointed hour. It seemed that nine o'clock would never come, and I spent the time walking up and down Chestnut Street. At last, trembling with suppressed excitement, I entered his studio, and met this most kindly old artist. His first question was, could I draw a straight line? I was like the man who was asked if he could play the violin. "He did not know but, if he could be given one, he would try and see." I tried and saw. For three hours, I drew, or tried to draw, simple straight lines, parallel horizontal lines, and parallel perpendicular lines. At the end of the time, dizzy and dejected, I paid my two dollars, and left completely disheartened—all my dreams of the morning smashed to smithereens. So this was art! So different from what I had imagined! But was it really art? *Could* it be? And, if so, could I ever become an artist? The chances seemed greatly reduced.

It took a couple of days to restore somewhat my depressed spirits. One thing was decided. If I should have to learn to draw straight lines, I should have to do it by myself.

So I plodded along as best I could without instruction, and I must have made some little progress; for, the next school vacation, while at Atlantic City, a sketch of a wrecked schooner driven ashore during a great storm, seemed to have enough in it to attract the attention of Mr. X——, an amateur artist, spending the summer at this place. I found that he was a man of most generous impulses, as well as most erratic in his likes and dislikes, and it was very probably the last-named quality that was the cause of my good fortune. He was like a father to me, only, however, requiring the complete renunciation of all ideas not in accord with his own.

Upon his return to Philadelphia, he received me into his home, where I lived and worked with him for over a year. It was, however, a most restrained life, as his every whim about art had to be most religiously followed. He was opposed to all academic study, and, whenever I expressed a wish to go to the Pennsylvania Academy of the Fine Arts, he always opposed. I have much to thank him for, though our acquaintance came to a rather sudden ending.

Dr. W—— visited the studio. In his natural, straightforward manner, this eminent physician showed in a marked degree his interest in what I was doing, without having, however, previously complimented the work of

Mr. X———. I felt most uncomfortable during this visit, as I saw at once that my benefactor was not pleased, and that it would mean several days of morose silence in which all my efforts to restore the *status quo* would be utterly fruitless. For some reason, I went home that evening, and upon my return the next morning I found all my belongings, with my little canvases tied together, outside his locked studio door. I made several fruitless efforts to see him and find out in what I had sinned, but without avail. I only saw him once again, several years afterward.

In the regular course of events I left school. When my good father, realizing how uncertain was the question of any special talent for art in me, and how uncertain the life of an artist might be, even if I had talent—which certainly was not yet demonstrated—put me with a friend to learn the flour business. But belief in myself did not fail, nor my ardor flag. To do any painting now, I had to be up with the dawn to seize the precious minutes of light before seven, when I had to be off to the humbler, though more useful, avocation of selling flour.

This work proved too trying for me, and a severe illness, from which I did not completely recover for many years, decided my family to allow me to be an artist— if I could.

I was only a lad of eighteen, and my art career was at last really launched. But I was beset by two pressing needs—the need of money and, by far the more serious, the need of health. It was easy enough to be advised to go to the Adirondacks, but how? That some change was desirable, and even necessary, cannot be doubted, so much so that, when my dear mother, who was used to my more or less delicate health, finally saw me off on my journey, she never expected, as she afterward told me, to see me return alive. But I did get there and returned alive, and I must always believe that it was the good God who opened the way and gave me good friends, thus filling me with confidence in the future which never deserted me in those darkest days.

Upon my return to Philadelphia, not a little benefited by this trip and one to Florida, I had the good fortune to make the intimate acquaintance of Mr. C. H. Shearer, an artist prominent in Philadelphia at that time. I can never too highly appreciate his personal service to me, and how his kindly nature and gentle disposition helped to reduce the bitterness I (at times) had in my life, and gave me a more hopeful view of my own individual situation.

About this time, Mr. Thomas Eakins, under whom I was studying at the Pennsylvania Academy of the Fine Arts, gave me a criticism which aided me then, and ever since; and, as it may apply to all walks of life, I will "pass it along." I had made a start on a study, which was not altogether bad, but very probably the best thing I had ever done. He encouraged me; but, instead of working to make it better, I became afraid I should destroy what I had done, and really did nothing the rest of the week. Well, he was disgusted. "What have you been doing? Get it, get it better, or get it worse. No middle ground of compromise." With this advice in my mind, I did all sorts of things. I purchased a goose, and from it made a picture. In fact, I became the owner of a sheep also, and made a sheep picture. To own a goose is bad enough, but do you know what it means to possess and try to educate in artistic habits a lone solitary sheep? Well, I will tell you something you never dreamed of, unless you have had my experience. While a flock of sheep is the personification of peace, docility, and all that is quietude, from my (unscientific) study, I have come to the conclusion that *one* sheep has none of the qualities of a flock of sheep, no, not one, except, it may be, their stupidity. One sheep is not "sheepish"; no, he is the most stubborn, balky, run-away, befuddled animal you can imagine. I have had other animals to serve as models, but never an animal that furnished so many alarms by day and night as that "peaceful" sheep. He was escaping from his stable (stable, by courtesy), breaking his tether, trespassing in neighbors' gardens, and eating down the very things they prized the most; or he was the very contradiction of all activity, refusing to be led to pasture

19

and causing a giggling crowd to collect as if by magic. To the question of those on the outside who could not see what was going on, it was: "Oh! it's Henry Tanner's sheep."

In spite of the difficulties, I got a sheep picture, and finally traded it for a pair of antlers, worth ten dollars.

I have had brilliant ideas in my life. One of them was to unite business and art. The thing to do was to have an occupation that would furnish a small income—a business that would not take all my time. So it was that I established a very modest photograph gallery at Atlanta, Georgia. The calculation that I should have some time was well made; the calculation that I should take some photos, a mistake. I had so much more leisure than I had calculated upon, and this so distressed me, that I could not work. So it turned out that I did nothing. I could neither make it go, nor dare let it go—because with "blood and tears" I got enough out of it to pay my board each week.

The "gallery" was sold. I was back to life. What had, perhaps, helped to make the situation more tantalizing was the fact that a picture of mine had been sold in Philadelphia, at an auction sale, for two hundred and fifty dollars; true, I had received but fifteen, but the incident had given me hope, and made me more than ever dissatisfied with the four or five dollars a week I was making in that miserable gallery.

Perhaps my most trying experience—trying in relation to my physical existence—was yet to come. It was, however, only bodily discomfort, and caused me little or no sighing. I had gone to Highlands, N.C., with the thought that with my camera I could at least make my expenses. I should be able to study, and at the same time the mountains would be good for my health.

I made photos of the whole immediate region, a most lovely country, and, as no photographer had ever visited it before, they were a success, and my hard times—very hard times—vanished as the mountain mists before the sun. In the fall, I was back in Atlanta, and for two seasons taught drawing, mostly to the teachers in Clark University. Among my very first commissions was a portrait of Professor Crogman. As I look backward now, I am sure he gave it to me to "help." I have never seen it since finishing, but I fear that, when I do, I shall want to replace it with one of to-day. This running across old pictures is a very trying thing. It runs both ways—you are either ashamed you did not do better, or surprised and ashamed that you do not now do better—both ways it is painful.

With some little money—a very little—laid by, I began again to think of Europe. I imparted this desire to Mrs. Hartzell, and it was arranged that I should have an exhibition of my pictures in Cincinnati, and see what could be done. So it was that, in the fall of 1890, all my hopes were centred in an exhibition which lasted two or three weeks. All that human effort could do was done by these good friends, but the gods refused to be propitious, and no pictures were sold. I would have taken twenty-five dollars for the pictures. The only part that seemed to have any value were the frames for which I had paid money.

That I should not be completely disheartened, my benefactors gave me a sum of money for my "entire collection," the amount of which I have forgotten. With this sum and a commission of $75 from Mr. E——, of Philadelphia, I set sail for Rome, via Liverpool and Paris, on the *City of Chester*, January 4, 1891.

Chronology

HENRY OSSAWA TANNER
(American, 1859-1937)

1859 Born 21 June in Pittsburgh, Pennsylvania; son of (later Bishop) Benjamin Tucker Tanner and Sarah (Miller) Tanner

1866 Family moved to Philadelphia

1872 Saw artist painting in Fairmont Park; motivated to begin himself

1880-82 Studied under Thomas Eakins at the Pennsylvania Academy of the Fine Arts

1882-88 Lived with parents in Philadelphia; attempted to become established as a painter; sold illustrations to New York publishers; work exhibited at the Pennsylvania Academy of the Fine Arts and at the National Academy of Design, New York

1888 Set up shop in Atlanta as professional photographer

1889 Taught drawing at Clark University in Atlanta

1890 Exhibition of paintings in Cincinnati

1891 Went to Paris

1890s Studied with Jean-Joseph Benjamin-Constant and Jean Paul Laurens at Academie Julien; joined the American Art Club

1893   *The Banjo Lesson,* genre painting (now at Hampton Institute, Hampton, Virginia)

1894   *The Music Lesson* accepted at Salon

1895   *The Young Sabot (Wooden Shoe) Maker* exhibited at Salon

1896   *Daniel in the Lions' Den* (now at Los Angeles County Museum of Art) exhibited at Salon; received an honorable mention

1897   *The Raising of Lazarus* exhibited at Salon; awarded a medal of the third class; purchased by the French government for the Luxembourg Gallery

1897   Traveled to Palestine; visited Venice on return

1897   *Portrait of the Artist's Mother* (now in the collection of Mrs. Sadie T. M. Alexander, Philadelphia)

1898   *The Annunciation* (now in Philadelphia Museum of Art, Wilstach Collection) exhibited at Salon

1898   Traveled to Holy Land; sketched and painted around Jerusalem and the Dead Sea

1899   Married Jessie M. Olssen on 14 December at Saint Giles-in-the-Fields, Bloomsbury, London

1899   *Christ and Nicodemus on a Rooftop* (now at Pennsylvania Academy of the Fine Arts) exhibited at Salon and at the Pennsylvania Academy of the Fine Arts where it was awarded the Lippincott Prize and purchased in 1900 for the Temple Collection

1900   *Christ Before the Doctors* exhibited at the Salon of the Société des Artistes Français

1900   *Daniel in the Lions' Den* awarded a silver medal at the Universal Exposition in Paris

1901   Awarded silver medal at the Pan American Exhibition in Buffalo

1902   Returned to United States

1903   Son, Jesse Ossawa, born 25 September in New York; purchased farmhouse for use in summer months at Trépied, near Etaples, in Normandy

1904   Awarded medal at St. Louis Exposition; returned to Paris

1905   Exhibited *The Good Samaritan and Christ Washing the Disciple's Feet* at Salon

1905	*Christ Convenanting with the High Priests* shown at Carnegie Exhibition
1906	*The Two Disciples at the Tomb*, transitional style, rich brown tones with blue areas, won Harris Prize for most distinguished work of art of season at Chicago exhibition; purchased by Art Institute of Chicago
1906	*The Disciples at Emmaus* purchased by French government
1908	*The Wise and Foolish Virgins* hung in Salon d'Honneur
1908	One man show of religious paintings at the American Art Galleries in New York
1909	Elected an associate member of the National Academy of Design
1910	Spent several months in Morocco
1911	One man show at Thurber's Gallery in Chicago
1914	World War I; Trepied evacuated; moved to England
1915	Awarded gold medal at Panama-Pacific Exposition, San Francisco
1917-19	Worked for American Red Cross in France
1919	Works included in an exhibition, "Group of American Artists," held at Knoedler Gallery in New York City and then circulated to several cities in the East and Midwest
1920s	Exhibited at Grand Central Art Galleries, New York City; continuing traditional themes and mystical feeling
1923	Elected Chevalier of the Legion of Honor
1925	Wife died 8 September
1927	Represented at exhibition of National Arts Club Galleries in New York where he received the National Arts Club bronze medal
1927	Elected a full academician in the National Academy of Design
1930	Received the Walter L. Clark prize for his entry, *Etaples Fisher Folk*, in the Members Prize Exhibition at the Grand Central Art Galleries, New York City
1933	*The Two Disciples at the Tomb* exhibited at Century of Progress exhibition in Chicago
1936	Final painting, *Return from the Crucifixion* (now at Howard University Art Gallery, Washington, D. C.)
1937	Died 25 May in Paris

Catalogue of the Exhibition

Dimensions are in inches; height precedes width.
Abbreviations.—JOT: Jesse Ossawa Tanner Collection
number; GCAG: Grand Central Art Galleries.
This is the first time an attempt has been made to date
Tanner's works and many dates are still a matter of
conjecture, as the artist often overpainted his work.
Unless otherwise noted, all loans are from the Frederick
Douglass Institute, Washington, D. C., Collection of
Mr. and Mrs. Norman B. Robbins.

Paintings, Watercolors, and Drawings

1. *Boy and Sheep Lying under Tree*,
   1881
   Oil on canvas, 17⅜ x 27, signed
   lower left: Tanner, 1881
   Provenance: Edward Lawrence
   Scull, Philadelphia.
   Mr. and Mrs. Henry W. Sawyer,
   III, Philadelphia

2. *Study of a Young Man*
   Conte crayon on paper, 12 x 9½
   Provenance: artist's collection;
   JOT 497; GCAG.

3. *Study of Negro Man*
   Conte crayon on paper,
   12½ x 10½
   Provenance: artist's collection;
   JOT 406; GCAG.

4. *Mountain Landscape, Highlands,
   North Carolina*, 1889
   Watercolor on paper, 10¾ x 15
   Provenance: artist's collection;
   JOT 809-B; GCAG.

5. *Mountain Landscape, Highlands,
   North Carolina*, 1889
   Watercolor on paper, 11 x 15,
   signed lower left: Highlands,
   North Carolina, H. O. Tanner
   Provenance: artist's collection;
   JOT 809; GCAG.

6. *Man Sitting in Chair*, 1889
   Conte crayon on paper, 15⅝ x
   11½, signed lower right:
   H. O. Tanner
   Provenance: artist's collection;
   JOT 819; GCAG.

7. *Sand Dunes in Sunset, Atlantic City,* 1890

7. *Sand Dunes in Sunset, Atlantic City,* 1890
Oil on canvas, 29¼ x 58¾,
signed lower left: H. Tanner
Provenance: Bishop and Mrs.
B. J. Tanner, Philadelphia.
Mrs. Sadie T. M. Alexander,
Philadelphia

8. *The Banjo Lesson,* 1893
Oil on canvas, 35 x 48½, signed
lower left: H. O. Tanner, 93
From sketches done in 1889,
Highlands, North Carolina.
Hampton Institute, Hampton,
Virginia

9. *The Young Sabot (Wooden Shoe)*
Maker, 1895
Oil on canvas, 41 x 35, signed
lower left: H. O. Tanner, 1895
Provenance: Bishop and Mrs.
B. J. Tanner, Philadelphia.
Mrs. Sadie T. M. Alexander,
Philadelphia

10. *Les Invalides,* 1896
Oil on canvas, 13 x 16¼, signed
lower left: H. O. Tanner, 96
Provenance: private collector;
Hirschl & Adler, New York City.
Mrs. Salim Lewis, New York City

11. *Return Home,* 1897
Watercolor on paper, 9⅞ x 13¾
Provenance: artist's collection;
JOT 803; GCAG.

12. *Kansas City, Kansas,* 1897
Watercolor on paper, 9⅞ x 13⅞
Provenance: artist's collection;
JOT 204; GCAG.

13. *Kansas City, Kansas,* 1897
Watercolor on paper, 9⅞ x 13⅞,
inscribed lower left:
Kansas City, Kansas
Provenance: artist's collection;
JOT 642; GCAG.

9. *The Young Sabot (Wooden Shoe) Maker,* 1895

14. *Portrait of the Artist's Mother,*
1897
Oil on canvas, 29¼ x 39½, signed
lower right: To my dear
Mother, H. O. Tanner, 1897
Provenance: Bishop and Mrs.
B. J. Tanner, Philadelphia.
Mrs. Sadie T. M. Alexander,
Philadelphia

15. *Mother of Henry O. Tanner*
oil, 14½ x 11½
Provenance: artist's collection;
JOT 29, GCAG.
Jesse O. Tanner, Paris

8. *The Banjo Lesson*, 1893

16. *Portrait of the Artist's Father*,
1897
Oil on canvas, 15 x 14, signed
lower right: A hurried study
of my dear Father, H. O. Tanner,
Sep., 1897, Kansas City
Provenance: Bishop and Mrs.
B. J. Tanner, Philadelphia.
Mrs. Sadie T. M. Alexander,
Philadelphia

17. *The Canyon*, circa 1897
Oil on canvas, 16 x 12¾
Provenance: artist's collection;
JOT 90; GCAG.

18. *Lions in the Desert*
Oil on plywood, 15⅝ x 29⅜
Provenance: artist's collection;
JOT 141; GCAG.

19. *Abraham's Oak*, circa 1897
Oil on canvas, 21¼ x 28⅜
Provenance: artist's collection;
JOT 139; GCAG.

20. *Study for Raising of Lazarus*, 1897
Oil on plywood, 6 x 7⅞
Provenance: artist's collection;
JOT 122, GCAG.

19. *Abraham's Oak,* circa 1897

23. *The Annunciation,* 1898

21. *Study for Mary,* circa 1898
    Conte crayon on paper,
    23⅛ x 13⅞
    Provenance: artist's collection;
    JOT 302; GCAG

22. *Study for the Annunciation*
    Oil tempera on board, 8½ x 10½
    Provenance: artist's collection;
    JOT 18; GCAG.

23. *The Annunciation,* 1898
    Oil on canvas, 57 x 71¼, signed
    lower left: H. O. Tanner, 1898
    Provenance: Philadelphia
    exhibition, museum purchase.
    Philadelphia Museum of Art,
    Wilstach Collection

24. *Profile of a Woman's Head,*
    circa 1899
    Oil, 14¼ x 11¾
    Warren M. Robbins,
    Washington, D. C.

25. *Study for Christ and Nicodemus*
    on a Rooftop, 1899
    Oil on wood panel, 9⅜ x 13
    Provenance: artist's collection;
    JOT 9, GCAG.

26. *Study for Christ and Nicodemus*
    on a Rooftop, 1899
    Oil on canvas, 7⅞ x 15⅛
    Provenance: artist's collection;
    JOT 23, GCAG.
    Merton D. Simpson, New York City

27. *Christ and Nicodemus on a Rooftop,* 1899

27. *Christ and Nicodemus on a Rooftop,* 1899
    Oil on canvas, 34 x 40, signed
    lower left: H. O. Tanner,
    Jerusalem, 1899
    Provenance: Pennsylvania
    Academy of the Fine Arts
    exhibition (Lippincott Prize),
    museum purchase, 1900.
    Pennsylvania Academy of the Fine
    Arts, Philadelphia, Temple
    Collection

28. *Head of a Jew in Palestine,*
    circa 1899
    Oil on canvas, 24 x 21⅛
    Provenance: artist's collection;
    JOT 140; GCAG.

29. *Flight from Egypt*
    Oil, 19¾ x 25½
    Thomas Loguidice, New York City

30. *Gateway, Tangier*
    Oil on plywood, 22¾ x 19½
    Provenance: artist's collection;
    JOT 144; GCAG.

28. *Head of a Jew in Palestine,* circa 1899

31. *Christ at the Home of Mary and Martha*, 1905
Oil on canvas, 50 x 39, signed lower left: H. O. Tanner
Provenance: museum purchase, 1906.
Museum of Art, Carnegie Institute, Pittsburgh

32. *The Three Marys*, circa 1905
Oil on canvas, 48 x 52
Fisk University Department of Art, Nashville

33. *Study for Disciple Kneeling at the Tomb*
Conte crayon on paper, 13½ x 9⅝
Provenance: artist's collection; JOT 630; GCAG.

34. *Study for Disciple Kneeling at Tomb, the Head*
Conte crayon on paper, 15½ x 15
Provenance: artist's collection; JOT 857; GCAG.
Merton D. Simpson, New York City

33. *Study for Disciple Kneeling at the Tomb*

36.   *The Two Disciples at the Tomb*, 1906

37. *The Savior*

35. *The Two Disciples at the Tomb*
    (Disciple Kneeling)
    Oil on board, 52⅛ x 43⅜, label
    on reverse: Exposition de
    Pittsburgh, No. 102, Tanner, H. O.
    Provenance: artist's collection;
    JOT 168-40; GCAG.
    Merton D. Simpson,
    New York City

36. *The Two Disciples at the Tomb*, 1906
    Oil on canvas, 51 x 41⅞, signed
    lower left: H. O. Tanner
    Provenance: Chicago Annual
    Exhibition (Harris prize), 1906,
    museum purchase.
    The Art Institute of Chicago,
    Robert Alexander Waller Fund

37. *The Savior*
    Oil on plywood, 29⅛ x 21⅞, on
    reverse of frame: Exposition de
    [Pittsburgh] No. 60
    Provenance: artist's collection;
    JOT G-4; GCAG.

38. *Study for Portrait of Mrs. Atherton Curtis*
Conte crayon on paper, 18⅝ x 20
Provenance: artist's collection;
JOT 812; GCAG.

39. *Portrait of Mr. and Mrs. Atherton Curtis with Still Life*
Oil on plywood, 26⅝ x 28¾
Provenance: artist's collection;
JOT 951, GCAG.

40. *Flight into Egypt (at the Inn)*
Oil on plywood, 22 x 18½
Provenance: artist's collection;
JOT 142, GCAG.

41. *Portrait*, circa 1910
Conte crayon on paper, 8½ x 8¼
Provenance: artist's collection;
JOT 407; GCAG.

42. *Hand*
Conte crayon on paper,
10½ x 13⅞
Provenance: artist's collection;
JOT 620; GCAG.

43. *Portrait of Harry Boddington*
Conte crayon on paper, 15 x 10⅝,
signed lower right: H. O. Tanner.
Inscribed upper left: Portrait
Harry Boddington
Provenance: artist's collection;
JOT 854; GCAG.
Merton D. Simpson,
New York City

44. *Head of Woman in Jerusalem*
Oil on canvas mounted on
cardboard, 17 x 13⅝
Provenance: artist's collection;
JOT 134; GCAG.

45. *Head of a Disciple*
Oil on pańel, 13¾ x 10
Provenance: artist's collection;
JOT 28; GCAG.

46. *Burning of Sodom*
Oil on canvas, 20⅜ x 36
High Museum of Art,
J. J. Haverty Collection, Atlanta

46. *Burning of Sodom*

49. *Angel Appearing before the Wise Men,* circa 1910

47. *Flight from Sodom and Gomorrah*
Oil on canvas, 41 x 53, signed
lower left: H. O. Tanner
Provenance: artist's collection;
JOT G-7; GCAG.
Haig Tashjian, New York City

48. *Salome with Head of John the Baptist*
Oil on canvas, 46 x 35⅛, signed
lower right: H. O. Tanner
Provenance: artist's collection;
JOT G-6; GCAG.
Grand Central Art Galleries,
New York City

49. *Angel Appearing Before the Wise Men,* circa 1910
Oil on canvas, 24⅝ x 31⅞, signed
lower left: H. O. Tanner
Provenance: artist's collection;
JOT G-5; GCAG.

50. *Street Scene, Tangier (Man Leading Calf)*
Oil on composition board,
10⅝ x 13¾
Provenance: artist's collection;
JOT 131; GCAG.

50. *Street Scene, Tangier (Man Leading Calf)*

51. *Sunlight, Tangier*, circa 1912
Oil on cardboard, 10⅝ x 13¾
Milwaukee Art Center

52. *Walls of Tangier in Moonlight*,
1914
Oil on canvas, 25 x 21, signed
lower left: H. O. Tanner
Los Angeles County Museum of
Art, Mr. and Mrs. William P.
Harrison Collection

53. *The Good Shepherd*, circa 1914
Oil on canvas, 20 x 24, signed
lower right: H. O. Tanner
Isaac Delgado Museum of Art,
New Orleans, gift of Dr. I. M. Cline

54. *American Red Cross Canteen,
Toul, France, World War I*, 1918
Oil on canvas, 25⅝ x 31⅞, signed
lower right: H. O. Tanner, Toul
Provenance: Red Cross
commission to artist.
American National Red Cross,
Washington, D.C.

55. *Intersection of Roads,*
    Neufchateau, World War I, 1918
    Oil on canvas, 25⅝ x 31⅞,
    signed lower left: H. O. Tanner
    Provenance: Red Cross
    commission to artist.
    American National Red Cross,
    Washington, D.C.

56. *A. R. C. Canteen, World War I,* 1918
    Conte crayon on paper,
    17½ x 22¾
    Provenance: artist's collection;
    JOT 837; GCAG.

57. *Flight into Egypt,* 1921
    Oil on board, 19½ x 24½, signed
    lower right: H. O. Tanner, 1921
    Museum of Fine Arts, Houston,
    gift of Mrs. Even W. Burris

58. *Christ and Disciples*
    Oil, 30¼ x 36½, signed lower
    left: H. O. Tanner
    Spelman College, Atlanta

58. *Christ and Disciples*

59. *Moses in the Bullrushes*, 192

61. *Daniel in the Lions' Den,* circa 1921

59. *Moses in the Bullrushes,* 1921
Oil on wood panel, 22¼ x 15¼,
signed lower left: H. O. Tanner,
1921
Provenance: artist's collection;
JOT 91; GCAG.

60. *Moses in the Bullrushes,*
circa 1921
Oil on panel, 18¼ x 15⅛,
signed lower left: H. O. Tanner
Provenance: artist's collection;
JOT 132; GCAG.
Carroll Greene, Jr.,
Washington, D.C.

61. *Daniel in the Lions' Den,*
1895—1921
Oil on paper on canvas, 41¼ x 50,
signed lower left: H. O. Tanner,
Paris
Los Angeles County Museum of
Art, Mr. and Mrs. William P.
Harrison Collection

62. *Etaples Fisher Folk,* 1923
Oil on canvas, 47⅜ x 38, signed
lower right: H. O. Tanner, 1923
Provenance: GCAG; J. J. Haverty.
High Museum of Art, Atlanta,
J. J. Haverty Collection

63. *Flight into Egypt*, 1928
Oil-tempera on board, 17 x 17
Warren M. Robbins,
Washington, D.C.

64. *Fishermen Returning at Night*,
circa 1930
Oil-tempera on board, 9⅜ x 7½,
notation on reverse: The varnish
wasn't . . . that the tempera when
put on cracked. Scraped off not too
well to put on again. Still some
cracks but will continue to see if
cracks can be eliminated.
Provenance: artist's collection;
JOT 31; GCAG.
Merton D. Simpson,
New York City

65. *Fisherman's Return*
Oil, 30 x 24, signed lower left:
H. O. Tanner
Provenance: artist's collection.
Jesse O. Tanner, Paris

66. *Return from the Cross*, circa 1930
Oil-tempera on masonite board,
10⅛ x 16
Provenance: artist's collection;
JOT 38; GCAG.
Merton D. Simpson, New York City

67. *The Good Shepherd*, circa 1930
Oil-tempera on board, 10⅝ x 8⅛,
illegible notation on reverse
Provenance: artist's collection;
JOT 53; GCAG.
Merton D. Simpson, New York City

68. *The Good Shepherd*, circa 1930
Oil-tempera on board, 9¼ x 13,
on reverse: 2 coats blanc
d'espagne, 1 of colle, rather thick,
color in tempera, varnished in
glue 10 per cent solution with
lanoline, 2 wks after washed color
with alcohol
Provenance: artist's collection;
JOT 33; GCAG.
Merton D. Simpson, New York City

70. *He Healed the Sick,* circa 1930

72. *Study for Mary Returning from the Crucifixion,* circa 1933

69. *The Good Shepherd (Atlas Mountains Morocco),* circa 1930
Oil-tempera on composition board, 29⅞ x 35⅞, signed lower right: H. O. Tanner. Inscribed on reverse: H. O. Tanner, Etaples, Paris, 43 Rue de Fluerons 6
Provenance: artist's collection; JOT G-2; GCAG.

70. *He Healed the Sick,* circa 1930
Oil-tempera on canvasboard, 16¼ x 21½
Provenance: artist's collection; JOT 143; GCAG.

71. *And He Disappeared Out of Their Sight*
Oil, 10¾ x 13⅞
Provenance: artist's collection; JOT 85; GCAG.

72. *Study for Mary Returning from the Crucifixion,* circa 1933
Conte crayon on paper, 15 x 14, signed lower left: Study for Return from the Crucifixion, H. O. Tanner, 1933
Provenance: artist's collection; JOT 420; GCAG.

73. *Study for the Disciple Peter,* circa 1933

73. *Study for the Disciple Peter*,
    circa 1933
    Conte crayon on paper,
    18½ x 14¾, signed lower left:
    H. O. Tanner
    Provenance: artist's collection;
    JOT 808; GCAG.

74. *Return from the Crucifixion*, 1936
    Oil-tempera on board, 18 x 23,
    signed lower right: H. O. Tanner,
    1936
    Howard University Gallery of Art,
    Washington, D.C.

74. *Return from the Crucifixion*, 1936

Engravings and Etchings

75. *Little Girls with Deer*, 1888
    Wood Engraving, 9¼ x 6⅝,
    from *Harper's Monthly*
    signed in plate lower right:
    H. O. Tanner
    Marcia M. Mathews, Atlanta

76. *Christ Walking on the Water*
    Etching, 7¼ x 9½, signed lower
    left "H. O. Tanner," signed lower
    right, Trépied, Xmas, 1913. Signed
    lower left: H. O. Tanner
    Provenance: artist's collection;
    JOT 6; GCAG.

77. *Mosque, Tangier*
    Etching, 7 x 9¼, signed lower
    left: H. O. Tanner
    Provenance: artist's collection;
    JOT 19; GCAG.
    Merton D. Simpson,
    New York City

78. *The Raising of Lazarus*
    Etching, 8½ x 6½, signed
    lower left: H. O. Tanner
    Provenance: artist's collection.
    Mr. and Mrs. Erwin S. Barrie,
    Greenwich, Connecticut

79. *Capsized Fishing Boats, Brittany*
    Etching, 6 x 7¾, signed in plate
    lower right: H. O. Tanner
    Provenance: JOT; GCAG.

80. *Gate in Tangier*
    Etching, 9⅜ x 7,
    monogrammed lower right: T
    [in circle]
    Provenance: artist's collection;
    JOT; GCAG.

Related Works

81. *Portrait of Henry O. Tanner*,
    1900, by Thomas Eakins
    (American, 1844-1916),
    frontispiece
    Oil on canvas, 24⅛ x 20¼
    Hyde Collection, Glens Falls, N.Y.

List of Awards

1895-1924	Chosen to exhibit each year	Salon des Artistes Français, Paris
1896	Honorable Mention	Salon des Artistes Français, Paris
1897	Third Class Medal	Salon des Artistes Français, Paris
1900	Lippincott Prize	Pennsylvania Academy of the Fine Arts, Philadelphia
	Silver Medal	Exposition Universale, Paris
1901	Silver Medal	Pan American Exposition, Buffalo
1904	Silver Medal	St. Louis Exposition
1906	Second Class Medal	Salon des Artistes Français, Paris
	Harris Prize	Art Institute of Chicago
1908	Place of Honor	Salon des Artistes Français, Paris
1915	Gold Medal	Panama Pacific Exposition, San Francisco
1923	Chevalier, Legion of Honor	Paris: French government
1927	National Arts Club Bronze Medal	Exhibition of National Arts Club Galleries, New York City
1930	Walter L. Clark Prize	Grand Central Art Galleries, New York City

List of Exhibitions

1888   Pennsylvania Academy of the Fine Arts, Philadelphia
1891   National Academy of Design, New York City
1892-93   Earle's Galleries, Philadelphia
1894-1924   Salon des Artistes Français, Paris
1890   Methodist Headquarters, Cincinnati
1900   Exposition Universale, Paris
            Twelfth Annual Exhibition of the Philadelphia Art Club
1901   Pan American Exposition, Buffalo
1904   St. Louis Exposition
            Exhibition of the Society of American Artists
1905   Carnegie Institute Annual Exhibition, Pittsburgh
1906   Art Institute of Chicago
            Pennsylvania Academy of the Fine Arts, Philadelphia
1908   American Art Galleries, New York City
            Carnegie Institute Annual Exhibition, Pittsburgh
1911   Thurber's Gallery, Chicago
1913   Knoedler's Gallery, New York City
1914   Anglo-American Art Exhibition, London

1915	Panama-Pacific Exposition, San Francisco
1919	Group of American Artists, Knoedler's Gallery, New York City
1920	The Museum of History, Science and Art, Los Angeles
1920-30	Grand Central Art Galleries, New York City
1921	New York Public Library, New York City
	Vose Galleries, Boston
1922	Tanner Art League, Dunbar High School, Washington, D.C.
1924	Grand Central Art Galleries, New York City
1927	National Arts Club Galleries, New York City
1933	American Artists' Professional League, Simonson Galleries, Paris
1933-34	Century of Progress, Chicago
1945	Philadelphia Art Alliance
1966	UCLA Art Galleries, Los Angeles
1967	City University of New York, Harlem Cultural Council, and New York Urban League
	Grand Central Art Galleries, New York City
	Howard University Gallery of Art, Washington, D.C.
1968	Grand Central Art Galleries, New York City
1969	Spelman College, Atlanta

Photographs and Documents

A few documents, medals, and photographs are in the collection of the artist's son, Jesse Tanner, a selection of which is reproduced below.

Bishop Benjamin Tucker Tanner and his wife, Sarah Miller Tanner parents of Henry Ossawa Tanner

Henry O. Tanner at 4 years of age

Henry O. Tanner at 20 years of age

Lieutenant Tanner on the French Front, 1914-1918

The artist at 50 years of age

Tanner's citation as Chevalier, Legion of Honor, awarded August 17, 1923.

List of Organizations

American Art Association, member 1897

American Art Club, Paris, member, 1891

American Artists' Professional League, European chapter, 1930

National Academy of Design, New York City, ANA 1909, NA 192

Paris Society of American Painters, member 1909

Société Artistique de Picardie, President

Société Internationale Peinture et Sculpture, Paris

Selected Bibliography

General Reference Works

Brawley, Benjamin Griffith. *The Negro Genius*. New York: Biblo and Tannen, 1966.

Cartwright, W. Aubrey. *Guide to Art Museums in the United States, East Coast-Washington to Miami*. New York: Duell, Sloan and Pearce, 1958.

Dover, Cedric. *American Negro Art*. Greenwich, Connecticut: New York Graphic Society, 1960.

Edouard-Joseph. *Dictionnaire Biographique des Artistes Contemporains 1910-1930*. Paris: Librairie Grund, 1934.

Fielding, Mantle. *Dictionary of American Painters, Sculptors and Engravers*. New York: James F. Carr, 1965.

Hourticq, Louis. *Harper's Encyclopedia of Art*. New York: Harper and Brothers, 1937.

Huddleston, Sisley. *Bohemian Literary and Social Life in Paris*. London: George C. Harrap & Co., 1928.

Larkin, Oliver W. *Art and Life in America*. New York: Holt, Rinehart and Winston, 1966.

Levy, Florence N., editor. *Who's Who in Art*. New York: American Art Annual, 1912.

Locke, Alain. *The Negro in Art*. Washington, D.C.: Associates in Negro Folk Education, 1940.

McGlauflin, Alice Coe, editor. *Who's Who in American Art*. Washington, D.C.: The American Federation of Arts, 1935.

Mallett, Daniel Trowbridge. *Index of Artists*. New York: Peter Smith, 1948.

Mathews, Marcia M. *Henry Ossawa Tanner*. Chicago: University of Chicago Press, 1969.

Porter, James A. *Modern Negro Art*. New York: Dryden Press, 1943.

Young, William, editor. *A Dictionary of American Artists, Sculptors and Engravers*. Cambridge, Massachusetts: William Young and Co., 1968.

Catalogues

Barrie, Erwin S. *Exhibition of Paintings: Henry Ossawa Tanner*. New York: Grand Central Art Galleries, 16 November-2 December, 1967.

Bhalla, Hans, and Edmund Barry Gaither, *Henry O. Tanner, An Afro-American Romantic Realist (1859-1937)*. Atlanta: Spelman College, 30 March-30 April, 1969.

Greene, Carroll, Jr. *The Evolution of Afro-American Artists: 1800-1950*. New York: City University of New York in cooperation with Harlem Cultural Council and New York Urban League, 1967.

———, and Warren Robbins. *Tanner Graphics and Watercolors*. New York: Grand Central Art Galleries, 4-25 June, 1968.

Locke, Alain. *Memorial Exhibition of Paintings by Henry O. Tanner*. Philadelphia: Philadelphia Art Alliance, 2 October-11 November, 1945.

Morris, Harrison S. *Illustrated Catalogue of Religious Paintings by Mr. Henry O. Tanner*. New York: American Art Galleries, 1908.

Porter, James A. *The Negro in American Art: One Hundred and Fifty Years of Afro-American Art.* Los Angeles: UCLA Art Galleries, Dickson Art Center, September-October, 1966.

———. *Ten Afro-American Artists in the Nineteenth Century.* Washington, D.C., Howard University, Gallery of Art, February-March, 1967.

Articles

"An Afro-American Painter Who Has Become Famous in Paris." *Current Literature*, volume XLV (October 1908), page 405.

"Annunciation; Painting." *Century*, volume LIX (April 1900), page 815.

Baldwin, E. F. "Negro Artist of Unique Power." *Outlook*, volume LXIV (7 April 1900), pages 792-796.

Barton, William E. "An American Painter of the Resurrection." *Advance* (20 March 1913), page 2011.

Burroughs, Bryson. "A Characteristic Painting by Henry O. Tanner." *Metropolitan Museum Bulletin*, volume XX, no. 11 (November 1925), page 275.

Caffin, Charles H. "Exhibition of the Society of American Artists." *The International Studio*, volume XXII, pages CCLXI-CCLXXII.

Canaday, John. "Negroes in Art: An Exhibition Examines 250 Years of Pictorial Social History." *The New York Times* (24 May 1969).

Cole, Helen. "Henry O. Tanner, Painter." *Brush and Pencil*, volume 6 (June 1900), pages 97-107.

Collins, William B. "Negro's Oil Painting Is Featured Work at Museum Yule Exhibit." *The Philadelphia Inquirer* (15 December 1967).

"Field Notes (obit.): Henry Tanner Dies." *Magazine of Art,* volume XXX (July 1937), page 456.

Fauset, Jessie. "Henry Ossawa Tanner." *The Crisis,* volume XXVII (April 1924), pages 255-258.

Ghent, Henri. "Art Mailbag: White is not Superior." *The New York Times* (8 December 1968).

Greene, Carroll, Jr. "Afro-American Artists: Yesterday and Now." *The Humble Way* (Third Quarter 1968).

―――. "The Afro-American Artist: A Background." *The Art Gallery* (April 1968), pages 12-25.

"Henry Tanner, 77, Dies in Paris, Was American Negro Painter." *New York Herald Tribune* (25 May 1937).

Lester, W. R. "Henry O. Tanner, Exile for Art's Sake." *Alexander's Magazine* (15 December 1908), page 69.

MacChesney, Clara T. "A Poet-Painter of Palestine." *The International Studio,* volume L (July 1913), pages xi-xv.

Mathews, Marcia M. "Henry Ossawa Tanner, American Artist." *The South Atlantic Quarterly,* volume LXV, no. 4 (Autumn 1966), pages 1-10.

"News and Comment: The Negro in Art." *The Magazine of Art,* volume 35 (April 1942), page 147.

"Notes: Henry O. Tanner." *Chicago Art Institute Bulletin,* volume 4 (July 1911), page 11.

Rich, Daniel Catton. "Fifty Years at Chicago." *The Magazine of Art,* volume 32 (December 1939), pages 704-709, 722-724.

Scarborough, W. S. "Henry O. Tanner." *Southern Workman,* volume XXXI (December 1902), pages 661-670.

Smith, Lucy, E. "Some American Painters in Paris." *The American Magazine of Art,* volume 18 (March 1927), pages 134-136.

Taylor, A. E. "The American Colony of Artists in Paris." *The International Studio,* volume XLVI, no. 184 (June 1912), pages 280-289.

Tanner, Henry Ossawa. "The Story of an Artist's Life, I." *The World's Work,* volume 18 (June 1909), pages 11661-11666.

―――. "The Story of an Artist's Life, II." *The World's Work,* volume 18 (July 1909), pages 11769-11775.

Thompson, Vance. "American Painters in Paris."
Cosmopolitan, volume XXIX (May 1900), pages 18-20.

Wuerpel, [nfn]. "American Artists Association of Paris."
Cosmopolitan, volume XX (February 1896).

Wyer, Raymond. "Art Collecting and Psychology." *The
International Studio,* volume LVIII (June 1916), pages
cxxi-cxxvi.

Selected Exhibition Reviews

Campbell, Lawrence. "Henry Ossawa Tanner at Grand
Central." *Art News,* volume LVIII (September 1968),
page 71.

Canaday, John. "Poor Deal for a Good Man." *The New York
Times* (19 November 1967).

——. "Postscript." *The New York Times* (3 December 1967).

Grafly, Dorothy. "Henry O. Tanner." *Pictures on Exhibit*
(October 1945), pages 14-15.

"Honoring Tanner." *The Art Digest* (1 October 1945).

"In the Galleries: Henry O. Tanner, N. A." *Arts Magazine,*
volume 42 (June/Summer, 1968), page 58.

Paris, Jeanne. "Tanner Show on Tuesday." *Long Island Press*
(2 June 1968).

Thompson, Vance. "Salon of 1908." *New York American*
(1 May 1908).

Index of Titles

Reference is to catalogue number. Asterisk (*) indicates illustration. Double asterisk (**) indicates illustration in color.